T0026469

MARTIN LUTHER KING JR.

Civil Rights Leader and American Hero

by Dr. Hugh Roome

Content Consultant

Nanci R. Vargus, Ed.D.
Professor Emeritus, University of Indianapolis

Reading Consultant

Jeanne M. Clidas, Ph.D.
Reading Specialist

Children's Press®
An Imprint of Scholastic Inc.

Library of Congress Cataloging-in-Publication Data
Names: Roome, Hugh, author. | Shepherd, Jodie, author.
Title: Martin Luther King Jr.: Civil Rights Leader and American Hero / by Hugh Roome ;
poem by Jodie Shepherd.
Description: New York: Children's Press, an imprint of Scholastic Inc., [2018] | Series: Rookie
biographies | Includes bibliographical references and index.
Identifiers: LCCN 2016057391| ISBN 9780531232279 (library binding: alk. paper) |
ISBN 9780531238615 (pbk.: alk. paper)
Subjects: LCSH: King, Martin Luther, Jr., 1929-1968—Juvenile literature. | African Americans—
Biography—Juvenile literature. | Civil rights workers—United States—Biography—Juvenile literature. |
African Americans—Civil rights—History—20th century—Juvenile literature. | Civil rights movements—
United States—History—20th century—Juvenile literature.
Classification: LCC E185.97.K5 R595 2018 | DDC 323.092 [B]—dc23
LC record available at https://lccn.loc.gov/2016057391

No part of this publication may be reproduced in whole or in part, or stored in a retrieval system,
or transmitted in any form or by any means, electronic, mechanical, photocopying, recording, or
otherwise, without written permission of the publisher. For information regarding permission, write
to Scholastic Inc., Attention: Permissions Department, 557 Broadway, New York, NY 10012.

Produced by Spooky Cheetah Press
Design by Judith Christ-Lafond
Poem by Jodie Shepherd

© 2018 by Scholastic Inc.

All rights reserved. Published in 2018 by Children's Press, an imprint of Scholastic Inc.

Printed in the United States of America 113

SCHOLASTIC, CHILDREN'S PRESS, ROOKIE BIOGRAPHIES™, and associated logos are trademarks
and/or registered trademarks of Scholastic Inc., 557 Broadway, New York, NY 10012.

2 3 4 5 6 7 8 9 10 R 27 26 25 24 23 22

Photographs ©: cover: Flip Schulke Archives/Corbis/Getty Images; back cover: Paul Schutzer/
Getty Images; 3 top: spawns/iStockphoto; 3 bottom: Bettmann/Getty Images; 4: AP Images; 8:
Buyenlarge/Getty Images; 10-11: Donald Uhrbrock/Getty Images; 12: pam koner-yohai/Getty
Images; 15: Afro Newspaper/Gado/Getty Images; 16: Harold Valentine/AP Images; 19: Bettmann/
Getty Images; 20: Bettmann/Getty Images; 22-23: AP Images; 24-25: Bettmann/Getty Images; 26-
27: SAUL LOEB/AFP/Getty Images; 29: AP Images; 30: spawns/iStockphoto; 31 bottom: Buyenlarge/
Getty Images; 31 center bottom: Donald Uhrbrock/Getty Images; 31 center top: Bettmann/Getty
Images; 31 top: Harold Valentine/AP Images; 32: spawns/iStockphoto.

Maps by Mapping Specialists.

Sources:
page 14: https://www.archives.gov/files/press/exhibits/dream-speech.pdf

TABLE OF CONTENTS

Meet Martin Luther King Jr.

Martin Luther King Jr. was a great American hero. He lost his life working to end unfair laws for black people. He said all people should be treated the same, no matter the color of their skin.

King was an important leader of the Civil Rights Movement.

Martin Luther King Jr. was born on January 15, 1929, in Atlanta, Georgia.

Martin grew up in the South. There were many **racist** laws there. Martin could not go to school with white kids. He could not eat at a restaurant with white people. He could not sit with them at the movies. That was just because Martin had black skin.

Life in the South was not easy for black people.

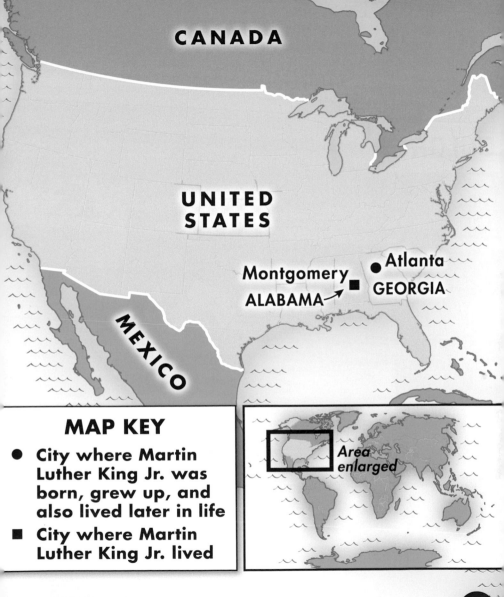

CANADA

UNITED STATES

Montgomery
ALABAMA

● Atlanta
GEORGIA

MEXICO

MAP KEY

● City where Martin Luther King Jr. was born, grew up, and also lived later in life

■ City where Martin Luther King Jr. lived

Area enlarged

This water fountain was for black people only. Many white people did not want to drink from the same fountains as black people.

COLORED

A lot of people had racist ideas, too. When Martin was 6 years old, he had a white friend. The father of the white boy said they could not play together because Martin had black skin. Martin said, "That is unfair!"

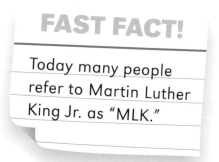

FAST FACT!

Today many people refer to Martin Luther King Jr. as "MLK."

Working for Change

King wanted to change the bad way black people were treated. He felt all people should be treated the same.

MLK wanted to change the laws that were unfair. He did not fight with his fists. He fought with words!

King speaks to the people in his church.

Here is King with his daughter Yolanda and son Martin Luther King III.

King worked hard in school.
He learned how to write
about the unfair laws.
He learned how to speak out
against racism.

King married Coretta Scott
in 1953. They moved to
Montgomery, Alabama.
In 1954, King became the
pastor of a church. He and
Coretta had four children.

Black people came to King's church to hear him speak. They wanted to learn how to change the bad laws. King believed people should never hurt each other. He chose peaceful ways, like **marches**, to fight for change.

FAST FACT!

"I have a dream that one day... little black boys and black girls will be able to join hands with little white boys and white girls as sisters and brothers."

—Martin Luther King Jr.

King is greeted by supporters (and his wife) in 1960.

Martin Luther King Jr.

King rides a Montgomery bus after the law was changed.

Leading the Charge

In Montgomery, black people had to sit in the back of any bus. If a white rider needed a black rider's seat, the black rider had to give it up.
King called for a **boycott**. Black people would not ride the buses until the law was changed. The bus companies lost a lot of money. The law was finally changed.

King used other ways to fight, too. He led thousands of people in marches. They sang songs about peace, freedom, and equality.

Many people saw the marches on TV. They heard King's speeches. His words made white people understand how racist laws hurt black people. Many Americans wanted to change those bad laws.

Martin Luther
King Jr.

King led many marches against racism.

Martin Luther King Jr.

Many white people marched with King to fight unfair laws.

In 1963, King led a March on Washington for Jobs and Freedom. He gave his famous "I Have a Dream" speech. About 250,000 people were there!

People of all skin colors joined King in his fight against racism. But some white people hated the changes that were being made. They fought MLK and his supporters.

King went to the
White House to
talk to President
Lyndon Johnson.
He asked the
president to help
change the laws.
Johnson said he
would help.

Martin Luther King Jr.

King and other black leaders meet with President Johnson.

23

President Johnson helped pass the Civil Rights Act of 1964. The law made it illegal to treat people unfairly simply because of the color of their skin. Every restaurant, store, and job would be open to *all* Americans.

People line up outside the Capitol Building to witness the Senate vote on the civil rights bill.

Giving His All

A white man named James Earl Ray hated the things King stood for. On April 4, 1968, he shot and killed King. The police found Ray and took him to jail.

FAST FACT!

Every year we celebrate Martin Luther King Jr. Day. It falls on the third Monday in January.

OUT OF THE MOUNTAIN OF DESPAIR,
A STONE OF HOPE

President Barack Obama tours the Martin Luther King Jr. Memorial in Washington, D.C.

Martin Luther King Jr. is a hero to people of all backgrounds and colors. He made our country a better place. He died to make life fair for *all* Americans.

Timeline of Martin Luther King Jr.'s Life

1929 **1954** **1955**

Born on January 15

Becomes a pastor

Gets unfair bus law changed

King waves after giving his "I Have a Dream" speech.

President Johnson signs Civil Rights Act

1963 **1964** **1968**

March on Washington for Jobs and Freedom

Killed on April 4

A Poem About Martin Luther King Jr.

He had a dream of equal rights
but used his *words*, not fists, to fight.
His message, in speech, or march, or strike:
Beneath our skin, we're all alike.

You Can Make a Difference

 Be kind and fair to all people—even if they don't look or talk like you.

 If you see someone being treated unfairly, tell a grown-up.

Glossary

- **boycott** (BOY-kaht): refusal to buy something or do business with someone as a protest

- **marches** (MAHRCH-es): large organized groups of people walking together to show their support of an idea

- **pastor** (PASS-tuhr): minister or priest in charge of a church or parish

- **racist** (RAY-sist): based on the belief that a particular race is better than others

Index

Facts for Now

Visit this Scholastic Web site for more information on Martin Luther King Jr. and download the Teaching Guide for this series:

www.factsfornow.scholastic.com

Enter the keywords Martin Luther King Jr.

About the Author

Dr. Hugh Roome is the publisher of Scholastic magazines *Let's Find Out*, *Scholastic News*, and *Storyworks*. He dedicates this book to Dr. Bernard Harleston, one of America's great educators, who has spent his life seeking equal opportunity for all.